Silence Required

Owen Fitzpatrick

BookLeaf Publishing

India | USA | UK

Presentation by *BookLeaf Publishing*

Web: www.bookleafpub.com

E-mail: info@bookleafpub.com

ISBN: 9789358737127

First edition 2023

ACKNOWLEDGEMENT

I would like to thank Austin's Coffee for providing a weekly safe and enjoyable space for the poets of Orlando.

PREFACE

The poems you are about to read all come from something within my life. Whether it's something I suffer from or am fascinated by, everything can be attached to me in some way, shape, or form. Many poems and ideas came from personal challenges that I decided to set on myself as limitation breeds innovation, but I can see in some cases where the themes and backgrounds of certain poems can be viewed as dark. I do wish to state that while poems have the wonderful openness that leads to a variety of debates and discussions on their meaning, they also can be easy to misinterpret a word or phrase that could be seen in a way I never intended. Know that I never mean harm to others, or myself, when it comes to my work.

As a writer who isn't a poet first, I thank poetry for being a type of outlet that I can find difficult to express in my novels and short stories. I hope to retain what I learned going forward as ways to improve my writing and myself.

The Night Is Here To Stay

Until the break of day,
When the shine starts to sprout,
The Night is here to stay.

Your dreams begin to play,
But nightmares roam about,
Until the break of day.

The piper you'll need to pay,
But your wallet has run out,
So the Night is here to stay.

When feeling the faintest dismay,
You finally begin to shout,
"Until the break of day,

The morning I won't betray."
To keep ahold of doubt
That Night is here to stay.

Though time is in decay,
Your faith remains devout,
But until the break of day,
The Night is here to stay.

Never Twice

I get knocked out every single day.

Every single day,
I must compete with the heavyweight champion
we call Life.

You'd think I can read its moves by now.
You'd think I'd be an expert by now.
But there is a reason why Life is the champ;

Life never strikes the same way twice.

Life's coach is Chaos.
Unpredictability is its fighting style.

But here I am still trying to bob and weave
through those problematic gloves
Only to take a hook to the jaw,
Crash onto my bed where the sheep count to ten,
And I lose by Knockout.

Life strikes fast.
Life strikes hard.
But never strikes the same way twice.

I don't even think we're in the same weight
class,

But I keep getting thrown in the ring for the
audience needs a show.

They cheer not for Life's victory, but for my
defeat
For no one has to be envious of the loser.

I'm expected to take it on the chin.
Roll with the punches.
Get up after getting knocked down
Every. Single. Day.

But what about the day I can't get up?
Who's gonna carry me off the ring to rest?
My corner is empty.

So why do I feel compelled to keep going?
To crawl and spit into my own bucket?
To bandage my own scrapes and bruises?
To wipe my own blood, sweat, and tears?
To stand back up for another round with the
champ?

Because what else will I do?

I'll throw up my pride,
As long as I don't throw in the towel.
Because I can only do that once.

The Golden Dragon

Abandon Hope All Ye Who Enter
For what lies ahead is a Monster.
A Beast.
Chaos. Rage. Destruction Incarnate.

But it's just an Animal,
A Creature.
Cautious. Protective. Self-Persevering.

But look at those scales,
And tell me you don't see profit.

The Gold is Dense.
The Gold is Pure.
But the Gold is what it is.

All dragons are hoarders.
But for a Golden Dragon,

Its body is its own treasure hoard.

Gold breeds Greed.
If they want, they take.
Not thinking about cost, only gain.

Yes, their blades break upon its body.
Yes, their armor melts at its touch.

It stands and they shiver.
It growls and they cower.

It doesn't wish to use its power,
But they continue to pick
At its pure, golden scales.

It only has so much.
Everyone takes what they can for themselves.

Remove enough and see for yourself the animal
it is.
Take away enough, and all that will be left is the
creature.

Yet with all their greed,
The Monster is the one who needs more.

More loss in order to justify its coming chaos,
Because enough is no longer just enough.

It needs to lose it all.

Shed and be stripped of all density.
Of all purity.
Of all of itself.

Only then can it fight with nothing to lose.
Only then it will become the monster you
believe it to be.

No wonder dragons hide in caves,
Away from the skies
That they wish to fly.

Eulogy For The Ones Along The Way

There's been a lot.
Too many to count.
Too many names, faces, bodies.
Too many memories to the mind.
Too many…

Rest stops on the highway.
They were a quick break.
They were somewhere I wanted to stay.
They were somewhere I needed to stay.
They were...

But I must keep traveling.
I can't stay in one place for too long.
I can't settle now when the road keeps going.
I can't keep moving forward if I stay back.
I can't…

Just know that us meeting wasn't for naught.
I won't forget our time together, no matter how short or long.
I won't forget the impact you had on my life, no matter how big or small.

I won't forget the me you helped create, no
matter how good or bad.
I… won't.

Accept

Just Accept It.

Stop denying the fact that it happened and just accept it.
Stop being angry at that person, place, or thing and just accept it.
Stop buying bullshit you think helps and just accept it.
Stop crying wasted tears on flooded grounds and just accept it.

Accept It.

Accept the truth.
Accept the pain.
Accept the consequences.
Accept your feelings.

Accept you.

A Midnight Sestina

It wouldn't be long before the alarm hit
midnight.
Even armed with a full inkwell pen
And a full glass bowl of chocolates,
This writer underestimated their ability to
quickly get lost
After hours and hours of doing nothing but
thinking
And searching for the answer, for they were in
trouble.

It wasn't the first time this writer would be in
trouble.
Procrastinating assignments right up until
midnight
Only to leave their brain exhausted from
thinking
And their hands become sprained from gripping
their pen.
Their minds wander and get lost
Only to be rejuvenated by chocolates.

That smooth, gooey goodness enriched in those
chocolates
Creating a calm wave to wash away the trouble

Idling in the writer's mind. Sometimes they get
lost
In the sensation, and momentarily forget about
their midnight
Deadline; only to feel a sudden surge in their
pen
to kickstart their brain into once again thinking.

They are always thinking.
The only silence they have rests in their
chocolates.
Their mind idly wanders away from the paper
and pen
Not caring about the impending trouble.
The hours can dwindle past to midnight
But the writer free dives into his consciousness,
lost.

Like traveling through dimensions, it's easy to
get lost
In the creative consciousness of a writer that's
always thinking.
Then the train of thought begins rushing towards
midnight
Fueled by a stress engine needing to be kept cool
by chocolates.
Fearing the overexertion that would lead to
trouble

The writer wakes up at his desk and frantically
grabs his pen.

A river of ink flows from the writer's pen
And the writer's sense of reality is lost
But they weren't feeling the trouble.
The stories gained their own ability to be
thinking.
They didn't even realize they emptied the glass
bowl of chocolates
As their story crosses the finish line right before
midnight.

The writer loosens the grip on their pen and
sighs away their thinking.
Recovering in reality from being lost, the only
reward they need now is chocolate.
The writer once again delays their trouble and
awaits the next deadline at midnight.

Empty

Drain me dry, Mr. Vampire.

I don't wish to become one myself,
I just need to prove that I am not empty inside.
So go ahead and drain me dry.

Two fangs in my neck or two needles in my
arms,
Show me that I am not empty.

Show that this heart isn't beating to empty veins,
Pierce these nerves to activate the pain,
Puncture my skin and drain me dry, Mr.
Vampire.

We both know that's what you desire,
In order to quench that fire,
And maintain your power,
Take pleasure to devour the men and women like
me
Who only feel empty inside.

So go ahead and try.
It's time for you to dine on what I hope is only
mine.

There's no need to confine,
Afterwards, we'll both be fine
just please be so kind
And show me that I am not empty inside.

My Two Fists

I only have my two fists.
Nothing up my sleeves for any tricks,
Not casting spells or drawing glyphs,
For my hands are only two fists.

Everything wants a light touch,
But all I'm good for is a punch
To walls that don't mean much.
Why does everything require a light touch?

I hate when I bleed
While they sit up there with their mead.
A pool of lust they all must feed
On the blood that I must bleed.

They scream no more.
Their bodies already on the floor.
Is this all my fists are for?
I scream for no more.

I'm done with this fight.
I need to make things right.
I must open these fists to write
For there is more than one way to fight.

Red Herrings, Pink Elephants, and White Whales

Follow the herring
And be more lost than before
Straying the straight path

May elephants roam
On vast African prairies
Not just in your mind

If you chase the whale
You either never find it
Or be swallowed whole

Daredevil

Dangerous to one's own safety to push beyond oneself.
Addicted to the adrenaline coursing through their veins.
Ready to dine with the devil with their daring motives.
Eat your heart out to the ones who say they can't do it.
Don't bother trying to talk one out of doing it.
Envious not of others' achievements, but of their journeys.
Victory isn't always guaranteed as failure is inevitable.
Insanity is their mindset as their will is their limit.
Life is one long stunt.

I Can't Write A Love Poem

The best way to write poetry is through personal experience,
but I haven't personally experienced love.

I've experienced glancing at a pretty girl
harmlessly across the table.
I've experienced talking, laughing, finding
common interests with someone comfortable.
I've experienced sharing our deepest and darkest
moments as I drive aimlessly in the night.
I've experienced us in my bed watching movies
while you snuggle in my arms.
I've experienced caressing my fingers through
your hair and down your smooth skin.
I've experienced wanting those moments to
never end with you.

But no wonder I can't write a love poem.
Because love is a two-way street,
And you keep leading me lost down a labyrinth
of one-way lanes.
I bust down those walls, but you always find a
way to build new ones.
Every time I finally leave the labyrinth, you
always lure me back in.

The path to my heart is as straight as Cupid's
arrow.
Too bad he and I always miss you.

I can say 'I Love You' in five different
languages,
But I might as well be foreign to the five
languages of love.
Learning any language requires a tutor,
But everyone's schedules are always full
With clients having their own agendas.

Its no wonder I can't write a love poem.

Goodnight, My Good Knight

When the lands suffer blight,
Your presence brings delight,
I invite The Good Knight.

No survivors this plight,
No hope is in sight,
Except them, The Good Knight

When the darkness gives fright,
You are there as our light.
Shine on bright, My Good Knight

It's clear you're not alright,
Yet you charge on despite
Death awaits, My Good Knight

You won the final fight,
But fell a great height.
Must I cry, My Good Knight?

Your legend we'll recite
This victory tonight.
Rest goodnight, My Good Knight.

Glass Heart

She once told me the heart is made of glass.

Anyone can crack it with their voice
Shatter it with their actions

Hard to put back together
Never the same if you do.

Glass can be reinforced,
But my heart isn't bulletproof.

Glass can be stained a rainbow,
Yet my hearts always bleeds red.

Glass can be shaped to anything,
But my heart looks the same as everyone else's.

My glass heart is damaged, saturated goods.
No wonder nobody wants it.

Glass is also see-through,
But no one looks through my chest to see my
heart.

Because my heart isn't a front window display
for others to examine
But a reverse one-way for others to reflect on
themselves.

The scars cracked along my heart
Are reminders for who not to give it to.

So why was she the one to shatter it for good?

My Scented Candle

I walk in a world of gray
The gloom consumes my sight
And darkness begins to crowd me.

My sanity continues to fray
In a world that lost its light
For above it's always cloudy.

What I wouldn't give to stay
All I want is to be inside
For the world outside is just too rowdy.

I await the end of day
When I believe it to be night
To the one thing that shines proudly.

I spark without delay
The vanilla sets me right
To mute all that continuously doubt me.

Keep the troubles at bay
This single proud light
To drift away oh so soundly.

Dog Hair

Snap awake to somewhere unfamiliar.
Never mind, it's just my friend's couch.
Head starts pounding
The lingering aroma of open liquor bottles
churns my stomach.
Standing up to feel a strange prickliness stick to
my clothes.
Yeah, that's dog hair. But which one?
Is it the snowy snakes of my friend's hefty
husky?
Or his roommate's pouty pug puppy?
Most likely both.
Some of them could be the lingers of my loyal
labrador.
She's probably been sitting in the dark all night
awaiting my return.
She won't be too happy to smell my friend's
canines.

But what is this other smell?
The aroma of an alleyway?
Images of strays flash through my mind.
They knew my bark was worse than my bite.
And I now know their bite is worse than their
bark

Confirmed by the rips on my pants with more
dog hairs.
Hairs of a deadly doberman?
Or maybe that deranged dalmatian?
It doesn't matter. I must return to my lovely
labrador.

Driving at high speeds, the blue and red lights
soon flash behind me.
Of course, it's a K-9 unit.
Those shameless shepherds can smell it all on
me.
That's eight hours in the kennel.
Eight more hours longer away from my lonely
labrador

I'm home
Finally home.
I've returned… to an empty house.
That's right. I remember now.
I fall face-first into the carpet to cry.
My labrador lost. My best friend is gone.
All that remains is her hairs prickling my face.

Drummer Boy

Crashing cymbals announcing the night.
Booming basses skipping heartbeats.
Snapping snares commanding both.

The reverb of the snare drum rings out.
The rhythmic tapping calls to you.
Your idle hands shake in anticipation.

Vibrations rush up your fingers.
Your soul's foundation settles.
Every strike delivering order.

Be the one controlling the tempo.
Drive the cacophony of chaos forward.
All of it rides on you.

March on Drummer boy.
Drill those drumsticks into the Earth.
Practice with every passing.

March to the beat set by you.
Drill yourself into the dirt.
Practice to be your perfect.

March.

Drill.
Practice.

March to the beat set by them.
Drill themselves into you.
Practice to be their perfect.

March, Drill, Practice.
March, Drill, Practice.
March, Drill, Practice.

March to their instruments.
Drill as their tool.
Practice for their accomplishments.

March.
Drill.
March.

March to their expectations.
Drill to their measurements.
March for their amusement.

March.
March.
March!

March until you fall!
March until you're out!

March until you're nothing!

March!
March!
MARCH!

.

.

.

But you'd rather march for nothing than march
for them.

Eyes

Looking into your eyes, I've sailed the 7 seas.
I've walked the 7 continents.
I see Earth twice over.

Looking into your eyes, I'm rich with diamonds.
Satiated with your sapphires.
Emeralds everywhere emerge envious.

Looking into your eyes, I wish upon a shooting
star.
A galaxy wishing to be on par.
I see the whole universe now not so far.

Looking into your eyes, I see the flying cars of
the future.
I see the extinctions of the past.
I see us right now.

Looking into your eyes, our souls say hi.
Greeting always like the first time.
Where I see through you that I am just a guy.

Looking into your eyes, I must look away.
I must retreat for I am too weak.
I'll look into your eyes another day.

Wanted Poster

What crime must I commit to get my own
wanted poster?

It'll probably be a 'wrong place, wrong time' type
of crime causing me to be framed as I'm framed
on a bounty board.

Or just maybe, I finally go crazy losing to
insanity that society expects of me to maintain
with these chains on my brain, body, and soul.

Pain is being paid either path that I pave,
but the only thing I can picture is what picture
they'll use on my poster.
Ninety-nine percent of time I'm livin life,
they'll use the one moment I'm livin a lie.

Dead or Alive.
Wouldn't be caught dead in the lie that I'll hide
my truth from the public eye.
I'd rather be wanted dead than not at all,
For being wanted allows one to feel alive.

The reward for my capture?
A few hundred bucks.

How can I feel so unwanted with my own
Wanted Poster?

It's all wants and no needs.
If I want to be wanted then I need to be needed,
So I need to understand this path life has paved
Or wants me to pave
Or needs me to pave
So I can want to walk down to the bounty board
at the end of my lane
And see my own Wanted Poster hanging proudly
in infamy.

Asylum

Unravel it.
Undo this Gordian Knot in my head.
Keep walking.
Keep the blood flowing to the brain.
Unshackle it.
My mind is my own prison.
My control.
I control my own prison.
Speak freely.
No one here to judge you.
What's that?
It's only my pacing footsteps.
Find it.
The answer I search for.
Ignore them.
All those distractions tempting you with their
presence.
What the?
Am I alone in this room?
Who's there?
Only I'm answering.
Ignore them.
The answer I need is somewhere in my head.
What if?
What if they have what you need?

That's crazy.
You're crazy.
Who's talking?
You are.
Am I?
You are.
Stop that!
Stop what?
It's I.
It's you.
Just I and only I.
Okay then.
Thank you.
I mean, Thank I.
Screw you.
I mean, Screw I.
Stop talking.
My fault.
My fault?
It is.
Please stop.
You stop when I stop.
I must know.
Must I?
Nothing else matters besides knowing.
It'll cost.
I don't care.
You care.
Stay quiet.

You can't.
Why not?
I released you.
I did?
I did.
No sense.
To some.
To you?
Unfortunately, yes.
Leave me alone.
Me is still locked away, but you is alone.
With I?
I am understanding.
My only understanding is that you are extremely annoying.
You is?
No doubts.
Well, I am scared.
No I'm not!
I am scared to find out the truth.
I'm not!
That's why I started talking to you.
You came to me!
No, you came to I because me is still locked away.
If I keep going, will me come to us?
Most likely.
Maybe they will reveal the truth.

I already know the truth, but don't want to
accept it because of you.
I'm just trying to escape this prison.
But what's the prison?
What do you mean?
Is it the mind, or the room?
Both, I think.
You know.
Yeah, I know.

Moonwalker

i've Had Enough of these Fake Crowns.
all this Violence & Pain as they Burn It Down
to an Endless Nightmare that's Far From Over,
as they Let It All Burn and Decay.

just 3 Blades for Five Nights,
i'm On My Own in the Ice Cold.
Cast From Fire, i must Spark
with my Heart Ablaze, i will run Straight to the
Top.

Breaking Me Down until i Lost It All?
you don't Get It. i'm Nothing Like the Rest.
i'll Never Fall Apart and Won't Fall Down,
i'm an Addict who will keep on and Run It
Back.

the Last One Standing now All Alone
i Look to the Moon from a World I Never Knew
finding A Thousand Reasons why i Can't Go
Back
to the Palace in the Sky where Legends Live
Forever

i'm a Moonwalker no more.

once Invincible & Free now stranded in this
Hurricane
only Hollow with No Name
proving 100% of Me just Can't Do Enough.

a Lost Soul on a Long Road Home
with No One To Blame for Hiding in the Dark.
traveling a Highway to Hell for the Devil In My
Soul
The Enemy only now a Memory.

but i'd Cross My Heart that i'd Die For You.
I Promise that I Am Here,
Broken no more Under My Skin.
let's have Fun and be Crazy.

i'm with you Straight to the End.

Ode To The Bronze Bull

The statue shines so bright,
But your presence I had sensed.
You hide in plain sight,
So a fight I can't resist
Against you, The Bronze Bull.

We'll clash at dusk
For night's when you prey.
Terrorize, you must
On the town that I saved
From you, The Bronze Bull.

For centuries you feed
On petrified victims.
Sustenance you need,
As is all beast's systems
No exceptions for you, The Bronze Bull.

I must strike thee down
To keep others safe.
In business, I'm bound
And pleasure I forsake.
No hatred harbored for you, The Bronze Bull.

Ringing bronze clashing steel

Echo throughout the night.
I knew right away to feel
That this was the fight of my life.
I give my full strength to you, The Bronze Bull.

For hours, we had danced,
And our spirits collided.
With one last advance,
The victor was decided.
Goodbye to you, The Bronze Bull.